To Deborah —

May you enjoy your most perfect union!

Carl Raschke
September 2023

Love

and the

More Perfect Union

D1478720

Love and the More Perfect Union

SIX KEYS TO RELATIONSHIP BLISS

Carl Frankel

MANGO GARDEN

KINGSTON, NEW YORK

TABLE OF CONTENTS

For Sheri and lovers everywhere

"We waste time looking for the perfect lover
instead of creating the perfect love."

—TOM ROBBINS

Acknowledgements

I owe my first debt of gratitude to my intimate partners over the years. I've had four major relationships (five if you include one in my early twenties that lasted a year and a half). I've learned an immense amount from these relationships, which have grown increasingly "conscious" with each new iteration.

I'm also grateful to the friends with whom I've shared my learning journey. For close to a decade, I was part of a men's group whose members beat me kindly upside the head whenever I needed it, which was often. Thanks, Steve L., Steve N., David, J-C, Mark, Tim, Rich, Norm and anyone else whose name escapes me.

I've also learned from the literature. Harville Hendrix, Terrence Real, Gayle Hendrix, George Pransky, David Schnarch, Marshall Rosenberg (whose specialty is non-violent communication) and Esther Perel—you are among my most admired trailblazers. This book stands on your shoulders.

Tilman Reitzle, thank you for your infinite patience, your unfailing good nature and for being, plus or minus a person or two, the best damn book designer in the galaxy.

Last but not least, I'd like to thank my partner, the sexuality teacher Sheri Winston. As I write this, we've been together going on eight years. It's been a passionate time and also more challenging than either of us would have wished for. Our clouds have had a silver lining, though: they've given us lots of opportunities to confront and get past old habits and wounds. Of late we've turned a corner. Our cup was half-full before. Now it runneth over.

In this, we seem to be mimicking the pattern described by Harville Hendrix and his wife Helen LaKelly Hunt, who had seven rough years before turning the corner and becoming relationship masters. *Love and the More Perfect Union* would not have been possible—it would not have been remotely possible—without what I've learned from and with Sheri.

Thank you, Sheri, for being my companion in life, in love, and learning. Thank you for being my creative collaborator and erotic inspiration. Thank you for the hot and wonderful Tiny Country we're creating.

CHAPTER 1:

A Short Book About Creating Lifelong Love

We can probably all agree: relationships are challenging. If there are partnerships where the couple's lives are strewn with flowers from the first to last day, they're the exception. For most of us, there are ups and downs, and times when we wonder why we're bothering at all.

Over the course of my sixty-plus years on this planet, I've been in four long-term relationships: a starter and in retrospect woefully clueless marriage (seven years), a twelve-year relationship with a mother surrogate, a nine-year relationship with a dear friend who described herself from the outset as "not really marriage material" and proved to know herself better than I did, and since 2005 with the sex teacher Sheri Winston, who, as a strong and independent being with a mind of her own, is a great partner for this project.

I wrote this book as part of a joint effort by Sheri and myself to remove painful conflict from our relationship and have it be consistently nurturing and ecstatic instead. I wanted my relationship with Sheri to be, at a deep level, the bed in which I lay me down to sleep.

With the help of the learnings that I've laid out in this book, we seem to have largely succeeded.

I didn't write this book only for us, though. I wrote it because I wish for other couples what I wish for us, and because my experience suggests the Paradise Project framework I lay out in these pages can work for many thoughtful couples.

* * *

I'm not a professional psychologist, nor am I a licensed relationship or sex therapist. I don't even play one on TV. I'm a writer, and this is a writer's book on relationships. One of the writer's abilities is to synthesize—at least, that's one of this writer's abilities. I've taken bits and pieces from different relationship experts and cobbled them into a scaffolding that is some of each and some of all and also some of me. Among the experts I've drawn from are Harville Hendrix (*Getting the Love You Want*), Gaye Hendrix (*Conscious Loving*), Esther Perel (*Mating in Captivity*), Terrence Real (*The New Rules of Marriage*) and David Schnarch (*Passionate Marriage*). Many of the relationship rules in this book are derived or lifted directly from one or more of these teachers.

Yet it's also the case that for all that I learned from them, none of these experts totally nailed it for me. I wanted a program I could follow easily amidst (and despite) all the inevitable distractions of ancient stories and daily living. It had to be simple—not too many moving parts—and memorable—constructed in a manner that would let my overburdened brain access the information on an as-needed basis, i.e., often. What I've tried to do here, in other words, is create a program that couples can actually do.

Ideally a writer will do more than synthesize. They'll also add their own insights. That was the case here. I was inspired to write this book by the relationship model that came to me over time that I call the continuum of connection. So far as I know, it's entirely original.

As a writer, I've found that the act of wrestling with the material can produce unexpected insights. This happened repeatedly here. For instance, somewhere along the way it occurred to me that the relationship literature I'm familiar with misses the mark in an important way. It fails to identify and give sufficient priority to an aspect of relationship that's like the proverbial elephant in the living room: every couple does it, no one talks about it. I'm not referring to sex, which most people these days are more than happy to discuss. I'm talking about culture-building. Every couple co-creates its own value system, its own laws and regulations, its own governance system, its own communication norms. *Are boys' (or girls') nights out okay? Is it okay to flirt or have intimate conversations with third parties? How about sex with third parties, as a couple or separately? How is conflict resolved? Who gets ownership of the remote control?* Relationships are comprised of a thousand little understandings, the vast majority of which just sort of happen—they're never deliberately debated or arrived at. Despite the subterranean aspect of much of the decision-making process, we're all founding fathers and mothers in our relationships, all in the business of culture creation.

Of Tiny Country Creation.

Here's a second example, which we can file under 'Really Important Principle of Happiness.' The basic principle is this: we're all in the chemical-manufacturing business. Negative thoughts and experiences produce feel-bad chemicals. Positive thoughts and experiences—like, for instance, laughter and learning and fun—produce feel-good chemicals. We "win" at the game of relationship—and life—to the extent that we produce feel-good chemicals. We "lose" to the extent that we churn out feel-bad ones.

It follows that, to prosper in their relationship—and in their lives—couples will do better by accentuating the positive. This is, among other things, a behaviorist operation. If we do as if, we eventually become as if. If we start actively seeking out the positive, pretty soon the positive starts coming unbidden to us. Partners in a successful relationship create a sanctuary that is built out of positive experiences. They become experts at generating feel-good chemicals and at not generating feel-bad ones. They become attuned to what

> **PARTNERS IN A SUCCESSFUL RELATIONSHIP CREATE A SANCTUARY BUILT OUT OF POSITIVE EXPERIENCES.**

produces positive and negative energy. They don't complain; they don't find fault; they don't fight. It's not that there are no grievances—every relationship produces grievances—but they have learned to apply conflict-resolution strategies that produce feel-good chemicals or at a minimum keep feel-bad chemicals at bay.

This—the Norman Vincent Peale principle; the magic of maintaining a positive attitude—is one of those truths that hides in plain sight. It's painfully clear once you see it. Until then, though, it's easy to draw on negativity as a source of energy. This is poison for relationships.

What This Book Offers

INTIMATE RELATIONSHIPS ARE MASSIVE, MURKY TERRITORY. They're crisscrossed by a tangle of motivations—lust, love, attachment, loyalty, necessity, and more. They're the heart of darkness and the heart of light, too. By their very nature, they defy rational analysis. We stumble into relationships and do our best to muddle through. For most of us, being in a relationship is like trying to drive from Albuquerque to Newfoundland without a map. These pages provide a compass.

More specifically, you will come away from these pages with four specific information sets:

• An understanding of the three core yearnings that drive our behavior in relationships.

• Insight into a paradox that is inherent in all relationships. We yearn to be autonomous and we also yearn to connect. The result: we're often out of synch with our partners, not to mention ourselves. Relationships require ongoing management of this tension.

• A visual map for understanding the dance of relationship and how to manage it skillfully. In the context of action, we humans thrive on concreteness. We benefit from clear mental maps. Yet, as noted earlier, we tend to navigate our relationships without them. By this map, there are five chambers in the house of love. In this book, you will learn what they are, how to identify which one you're in, and how to migrate to one that feels better.

- The understanding that, as noted earlier, the work of relationship includes Tiny Country Creation.

About This Title

UNTIL THE LAST MINUTE, THE TITLE OF THIS BOOK was *The Paradise Project: Love and the More Perfect Union*. This was how I'd initially conceived of the book and the title made sense to me. I saw (and still see) the work of relationship as a "Paradise Project." In the depth of our beings, we dream of a perfect connection with a Beloved. We long for an earthly paradise of two and it's in relationship that we try to achieve it.

I wrote this book in part because it was clear to me that in the context of relationships, we need to re-envision our notion of paradise. We need autonomy along with intimacy, and so paradise on this mortal plane isn't about the linear pursuit of more and more connectedness. It's more of a helmsman's operation, one that requires partners to navigate the tension between competing forces—the winds of autonomy and the currents of connection.

More dance, less direction.

And yet there remains direction. Even the most dedicatedly quarrelsome among us will agree that domestic harmony is better than disharmony. And so, while we're managing the wind and waves of autonomy and connection, we also want to be sailing toward a port. The port of domestic tranquility.

Paradise in the context of relationships is a nuanced concept. One reason I felt inspired to write this book was to communicate these subtleties, which are still at the heart of this book.

As for the 'Project' part, that's there to remind us that we don't get to paradise by flipping a switch. It requires hard work over time.

'Project'" had a second connotation, too. In those moments when the waters are roiled and paradise seems unattainable, the word was to serve as a reminder that every undertaking has its ups and downs.

'Project' is the grizzled baseball manager telling his squad, "It's a long season. Hang in there."

Late in the design phase, some advisors raised doubts about the commercial merits of the title. They were concerned that it might not be immediately obvious to a casual observer that The Paradise Project: Love and the More Perfect Union was about relationships. A brief dance between art and commerce ensued. When it was done, the mix had shifted and we had the title you now see on the cover.

The book itself hasn't changed, though. It's still built around the concept of a Paradise Project. You will find references to it throughout the book. The only change is that this theme is now absent from the title.

The marketing gods giveth and the marketing gods taketh away.

As for the former sub-title and now main title, Love and the More Perfect Union, it's derived from the Preamble to the US Constitution:

We the People of the United States, in order to form a more perfect Union, establish Justice, insure domestic Tranquility, provide for the common defense, promote the general Welfare, and secure the Blessings of Liberty to ourselves and our Posterity, do ordain and establish this Constitution for the United States of America."

The founding fathers were no dummies. They weren't trying to create a "perfect union." A "more perfect union," an improvement on the status quo, would do just fine, thank you very much. A similar humility seems appropriate for relationship aspirations. Continuous improvement is a realistic goal.

There's a paradox here. The Paradise Project never actually gets us to paradise, if we understand paradise as an ongoing state of perfect bliss. So long as we wear this mortal coil, we'll always be on the road: we'll never permanently "arrive." There's a flip side to this, though. To the extent that we can secure more "domestic Tranquility"—in other words, learn to get along with our partner, ideally with large doses of intimacy thrown in—

we increase the likelihood that moments of perfect connection will occur. Thus we do make paradise possible—but it's paradise in passing, paradise in transient spells of blinding beauty. Until enlightenment embraces us, the most we can hope for is the occasional visit, not permanent immersion.

One of the main purposes of relationship is to optimize the conditions that make possible these 'day trips' to paradise.

As suggested earlier, we do this through the hard work of Tiny Country Creation. This is the final point of the title, with its echo of the Founding Fathers and the Constitution's reference to domestic tranquility. Most relationships are unconscious, even anarchistic. Unconscious because they build off what our parents did, our culture instructs or our buried selves demand. Anarchistic because there's little or no structure to how decisions are made and power dynamics are played out—things just sort of happen.

We can never surface everything. We can't entirely strip the anarchy out of relationship either, nor should we aspire to. The rational mind will always be a cork bobbing on uncharted waters. We can make things more conscious and less anarchistic, though, by creating relationship rules—Tiny Country "laws"—that encourage some behaviors and discourage others. These rules can make the difference between a relationship that works and one that doesn't. We do this by being as conscious as possible in our roles as founding fathers and mothers of our private—and hopefully more perfect—union.

What Awaits You

Love and the More Perfect Union contains four chapters and two Appendices:

Chapter 1: A Short Book About Creating Lifelong Love. You've already read this: no need to elaborate.

Chapter 2: The Pillars of Relationship. We review the three foundational yearnings that drive us—autonomy, connection and equity.

Chapter 3: The Continuum of Connection. We lay out a visual map that takes us from the hell of total isolation to the heaven of perfect connection. This model helps us understand what we seek in relationship and how we get it.

Chapter 4: You Must Remember This. Relationships require simple, memorable guidelines. Most of us can remember six keys--and that's what you get here, the six keys of the sub-title.

Appendix A: Continuum of Connection Chart. A table summarizing the chief characteristics of the 'rooms' on the continuum of connection.

Appendix B: Practices and Techniques. A compendium of strategies and tactics Sheri and I have developed to help us navigate the shoals of relationship.

Working with the Paradise Project model has been a fun and fruitful experience for me. I hope you'll find it rewarding, too.

Now let's get going!

CHAPTER 2:

The Pillars of Relationship

WE BRING THREE FOUNDATIONAL NEEDS INTO OUR INTIMATE RELATION-
SHIPS. There's an easy-to-remember acronym for these yearnings: "A-C-E,"
for autonomy, connection and equity. They're important to know about
because they are essential components to every relationship, and also because they're integral to the "visual map" material that follows. You can't
tell the players without a scorecard, and you won't understand this book
without this foundational information.

Autonomy

We all have a longing to be separate. At about six months, we begin to
individuate. We start to learn that there's an "other" that's separate and
distinct from the self. While one of the responses can be existential rage of
the infantile variety—how dare the universe not give me absolute power!—
there's also a welcome aspect to this discovery. There's power in knowing
you can do things independently.

The terrible twos and the year or two following are all about individuation, all about breaking away from mother and asserting your autonomy.
"No and you can't make me," temper tantrums—these are tests of how
much self-assertion the toddler can get away with.

Despite its exploratory defiance, the toddler doesn't actually want un-
qualified separation. Typically the child wanders just beyond the "Mom
Zone," takes bold action of the two-year-old variety and then hurries back
for reassurance.

This going and coming is recapitulated throughout our lifetimes. We go out into the world of autonomy, individuation and relative separation, then return to the intimate bond of the dyad where—in theory, anyway—we feel safe and loved. A true story from a supermarket: a three-year-old is throwing a tantrum. "I hate you, Mom! Go away!" he hollers so everyone can hear—and then adds a crucial afterthought: "And take me with you!"

We recapitulate this saga throughout our lives. We want to be on our own; we want to be individuated; but we want our Beloved to be there, too. We want a sanctuary to return to. This is the stuff of epic literature, too. In Tolkien's *Lord of the Rings* trilogy, Frodo Baggins leaves the idyllic community of The Shire and goes out into the Big Bad World where he overcomes monumental challenges. And then, at the end, he comes home. It's the primal "toddler ventures outside the Mom Zone" story, with orcs and elves thrown in.

Autonomy is not a standalone concept. It's always pursued in the context of relationship: it requires a dyad by definition. To the solitary wolf-child in the forest, freedom is absolute, but autonomy is irrelevant. Autonomy vis-à-vis what? Your basic baby is different, though. The infant seeks bliss at mommy's breast—the paradise of perfect connection. A year or two later, the child, now a toddler, wanders boldly off into the next room, recapitulating as a Great Adventurer where every toddler has gone before. He then hastens back to mommy's skirt before setting out again.

Autonomy takes two. Always.

Connection

Just as we long to be separate and individuated, we also long to feel bonded to another person. We yearn to feel seen, heard, known. We want the boundaries between people—physical, emotional, energetic—to dissolve. We want to feel connected.

This is very primal, too—think Madonna and child, or baby at the breast. How much we're held as infants has a powerful influence on our long-term happiness: if we don't get enough of this nurturing touch, we tend to internalize this deficit as indicating we're unworthy of love. It's also essential to physical survival—infants who aren't touched have significantly higher mortality rates than those who are. When an infant is at the breast, it's getting both physical sustenance and emotional nurturance. No formula, no matter how packed with nutrients, can provide this. It's the entire mommy package that delivers the goods: the adoring eye contact, the cooing sounds, the rocking and holding, the perfect food and delivery system.

The mother-infant bond delivers another message, too—safety. An infant on its own is totally helpless. A ten-pound baby that can't roll over, much less fight back or run away, is a meal not on wheels for a predator. Attachment means, "There's someone watching over me." Literally.

The need for attachment is so primal that people time and again choose a bad relationship over no relationship at all, as with the tragically familiar saga of people who remain in relationships with abusive partners. When the partner is loving, the person becomes attached, and when the abuse occurs, the person takes it because, for them, bad strokes are better than none at all.

A fascinating study in childhood development called the Still Face Project powerfully captures the horror that comes with rupture of the dyad. In this study, the researcher, Edward Tronick, had a healthy, loving mother interact with her approximately six-month-old baby. The child would gurgle, mom's eyes would get big and she'd make a funny face back at her baby, the baby would smile and waggle its head and so on, in the lovely, loving dance of connection we all know. And then, in the experiment, there came a time when, at Tronick's direction, the mother turned away and, when she returned her gaze to the child, remained totally impassive. No affect whatsoever. The baby worked its entire repertoire of moves in an attempt to elicit a reaction. She pointed. She smiled. She giggled. She made a face. She did all the things she had done before to good effect, but this time she got nothing back at all. The infant's emotions went from playfulness to bewilderment to anger to total hysterical distress in under a minute.*

Autonomy: good. Aloneness: awful. Autonomy means there's a mommy in the background to come home to. Aloneness means there is no mommy, no all-protecting God or Goddess, and that saber-toothed tiger will get us.

The moral of the story is we crave attachment. This is a problem when we choose problematic partners, but it has an upside, too. Sometimes it's our need for attachment that keeps us hanging in there when our fight-or-flight impulses are screaming at us to run. Sometimes it's our need for attachment that sees us through to better days.

Connection and autonomy are competing impulses. When we're seeking autonomy, we're not all that interested in connection: it's not easy to have fun and exciting adventures when we're locked onto Mommy's nipple. Nor, when we're feeling connected, does autonomy have all that much appeal. Solitary explorations can't compete with the Almighty Tit when that divine connection is what you're after.

Give me liberty or give me breast.

Equity

Let's turn now to the "E" in the A-C-E equation—equity. Because it's an abstract, somewhat high-falutin concept, this may not strike you as a likely companion for autonomy and connection. So let's think of it instead as fundamental fairness.

Relationships have a sibling dynamic as well as a parent-child one—and is there any sibling cry more plaintive than, "No fair to me!"? *Joey got the extra cookie. Jill got a bicycle for Christmas and all I got was this dumb Nintendo.* Underlying this concern, of course, are more fundamental questions: Am I getting my fair share of love? Am I loved as much as my rival? And, more fundamentally still: am I worthy of being equally loved? Do I rate?

---

* The research project was terminated early out of consideration for the suffering of the infants.

He has one job and I have two. I'm the one who does all the shopping. I give lots of oral sex but never get any. Grievances like these can build up over time and create real unhappiness. If I feel that I'm getting the short end of the fairness stick in my relationship, I will inevitably grow resentful and this anger will show up in ways that undermines the relationship. I may go on the attack. I may withdraw. I may get all trigger-y and reactive. Regardless of the specifics of my response, there will be fractures in the relationship foundation.

Fairness and equality are bound at the hip. I'll illustrate this with an extreme example. On the fringes of society, there are couples who choose to live out a 24/7 master-slave relationship. They take their kinky play out of the bedroom and import it into the rest of their lives. Jill is a full-time mistress, Pat a full-time slave. Even in extreme cases like this, there is equity because Joe and Pat entered into this agreement as equal partners with an equal say in how they would play out their relationship. Thus even dramatically unbalanced relationships are premised in fundamental fairness. If not, by definition they're abusive.

Fairness covers more territory than you might think. Consider, for instance, integrity. If Cynthia is cheating on Sally, she's withholding important information from her partner. This is fundamentally unfair because Sally has a right to make informed decisions about her relationship and Cynthia's secrecy denies her that right. Transparency about important relationship matters is fundamentally fair. Withholding is not.

Fairness issues aren't easy to discuss. For one thing, they're inherently inflammatory. It's easy for the person on the receiving end to hear them as an accusation of selfishness, or as a felony-level charge that a basic covenant of relationship—that the partners shall love and care for each other—has been violated. They also put the person who's speaking up at risk. Complaining about unfairness can come across as petty whining.

Fairness issues are also difficult to quantify. Given all the ways partners take care of each other, how are we supposed to add it all up and determine who's getting the extra cookie, and how many? Fundamental fairness isn't the sort of thing you determine by putting debits and credits on a ledger. How do you compare doing the shopping against picking up the kids at school or doing carpentry tasks around the house? How do you factor in the special allowance that arises out of caring and commitment? Ivan does the lion's share of the household work, but Maurice has a physical infirmity, so he'll accept that extra burden. Does this entitle Ivan to preferential treatment in another relationship area such as maybe more sexual favors? Or perhaps he chooses to take on an extra share of the responsibilities because it's one way he expresses his love for Maurice— it's a 'gift of service.' Yet there may come a time when he's in a less generous mood and starts wanting a quid for the quo of what he gives. Is this inappropriate? Is it re-writing the contract after the fact and thus 'cheating?'

> EVERY COUPLE MUST DECIDE FOR THEMSELVES WHAT'S FAIR AND NOT FAIR IN THEIR PRIVATE TINY COUNTRY.

There aren't right answers to these questions: every couple must decide for themselves what's fair and not fair in their private Tiny Country. What's clearly a bad idea, though, is to pretend these issues don't exist. They do in every relationship, and it's usually better to address them.

So how do you do a fairness reckoning? The important thing to remember here is that discussions about fairness aren't left-brained, courtroom-like procedures where evidence is presented followed by a judicial ruling. Ultimately, they're about feelings. When the complainant is heard empathetically, that can make all the difference—and of course the outcome will be even more satisfactory if behavioral adjustments occur, too. These conversations are about "airing" as much as "fairing."

One of the key tests of a partner's appropriateness is if they are fundamentally fair about fundamental fairness. Do they genuinely want equality or do they have an abiding need for that extra cookie? If they are fundamentally biased towards "more for me," you'll be constantly swimming upstream against their will to power. This may or may not be worth it.

The Need to Cleave

There's a natural opposition between autonomy and connection. On the one hand, we long to merge with the Other—and this is an Other with an upper-case O because what we're ultimately longing for is to end the primal split between self and not self. Yet we also long to be free and separate, in other words, autonomous. This drive, too, is recapitulated throughout our lives. As we've seen, this is the Way of the Toddler, a path to independence that ideally includes a sanctuary to come home to.

Philosopher Ken Wilber provides a useful shorthand for differentiating between these two vectors by describing one as 'eco'—the desire to be connected and in community—and the other as 'ego'—the urge for self-assertion of the autonomous self.

Eco and ego, different stations on the circuit of the self that we ride throughout our lives.

The tension between these yearnings is captured in a 'contronym,' a word with opposing meanings. When we cleave to someone, we cling to them. We're attached to them. But we also use a cleaver to cut a single side of beef into multiple pieces. Cleave describes the yearning to be close and the act of creating separation.

So there you have it, in a one-word nutshell. We are the being that needs to cleave.

Despite the natural tension between them, the desires for connection and autonomy aren't incompatible. They can co-exist perfectly well. We can cleave in the connection way today and the autonomy way tomorrow. It's easy to lose sight of this, though, and view the two as incompatible.

Negative stories around autonomy and connection can feed this confusion. Consider, for instance, the "autonomy as a betrayal of connection" narrative. According to this story, my impulse for autonomy reflects a rejection of the primary relationship, or alternatively a fear that my partner will view it as expressing my desire to cut the ties of connection. Disloyal! If we track this back to its origins in toddler time, we find the toddler's pursuit of autonomy accompanied by anxiety—not the healthy anxiety of the adventurer who doesn't know what's around the next corner, but the unhealthy anxiety that the child's forays into independence will be taken badly by the primary love object and lead to rejection and abandonment.

Autonomy = disloyalty = abandonment = a date with a saber-toothed tiger.

People with activated "autonomy as a betrayal of connection" stories have two basic ways to deal with this anxiety. They can suppress their desire for autonomy or they can get stealthy about it. The first path feeds what I think of as the Romantic Fallacy—the notion that the goal of relationship is to have a 24/7 intimate connection. The good news about this approach is that it reduces the anxiety. If an emotion—in this case, the desire for autonomy—is off the table, then not only will you not be exposed to it, there's even a cultural imprimatur that says you shouldn't feel it. Talk about a weight off your shoulders!

The bad news, of course, is that you'll have to deal with the suffering caused by your suppressed desire for autonomy. Overall it's an unhealthy solution.

As for the stealth route, a modicum of privacy in the service of autonomy is a good thing. However, a healthy respect for the private sphere can easily slipslide into excessively secretive behavior. Pulling off the highway on the commute home to enjoy a private moment with the sunset is innocuous. Stopping at the local bar for a quick pop before heading home without telling one's partner may or may not be a relationship violation. Having an illicit affair because it feeds one's sense of autonomy is over the line if for no other reason than, as we've seen, it's fundamentally unfair to one's partner.

There are good and bad secrets. When we're being driven by the "autonomy as a betrayal of connection" story, the line between the two can get muddy.

There are also twinned "connection infringes on my right to autonomy" and "autonomy infringes on my right to connection" stories. Here, autonomy and connection are seen as locked into a zero-sum game where more of one means less of another. Let's say Paul wants to have a boy's night out at the bar, and his partner Mary wants an intimate night at home and proposes a game of strip poker. Early in their relationship, Paul would have been thrilled at her suggestion. What a hot way to spend an evening together! Now, however, it's just in the way. *I already spend so much time with Mary. And I know what her body looks like. Why is she trying to deny me an innocent night out with my friends?* As for Mary, she might be thinking, *I need intimate, sexual connection and Paul wants to go out partying with his friends instead of playing a fun, sexy game with me. What does that say about his desire for me and to be with me?*

Guilt drives the "autonomy as a betrayal of connection" story. *I'll be punished for my desire for autonomy.* Anger drives the infringement narratives. *Son-of-a-bitch doesn't care for me! Bitch be in my way!* Connection as infringement of autonomy

How does one undo the pernicious effects of these misbegotten stories? More broadly, how does one cultivate a relationship that fully embraces both autonomy and connection?

It helps immensely if we can surface our problematic stories about autonomy and connection—after all, you can't fix something if you don't know it's broken. Conversely, if I know that my story about autonomy and connection is getting in my way, I can work to re-write my script, ideally in collaboration with my partner.

We can also share activities that support autonomy and connection in equal measure. Like, for instance, great sex, which comes in two flavors— sacred and profane.* With sacred sex, we seek to dissolve the boundaries that keep people separate: it's about union. In the Tantric tradition, the union we seek isn't solely (or merely) between individuals: it's about union with the Divine. The Infinite.

With profane sex, we're not seeking divine union. We're seeking to have a hot and fabulous time with our partner. With great profane sex, we

---

* As used here, "profane" has no negative connotations. It doesn't mean sacrilegious or dirty. It simply means not sacred.

fully express our autonomy. There's a wild freedom in these encounters: we give ourselves and our partner permission to test the limits of our pleasure and also to be consensually transgressive. *Go ahead and scream, even though it's simply not done! Go ahead and be the bad girl you're not supposed to be! Don't worry about being considerate, just go ahead and 'use' me!*

Yet at the same time as we're embracing our autonomy, we're also sharing with our partner. We're connecting, indeed profoundly connecting, although not in the boundary-dissolving way that's associated with sacred sex. We're traveling out to the antipodes of our autonomy together: we're celebrating our autonomy together. We're getting to have our connection and autonomy too.

These dual autonomy/connection experiences don't only happen in the bedroom. If we go to a movie together and both have a positive experience in the relative solitude of the dark theater, then come out into the lobby afterward and discover that we both enjoyed it immensely, we're getting both autonomy—our private viewing experience—and connection—we're finding a common bond. Any time we go out into the world together, any time we have "adventures" together, it's potentially a celebration of both autonomy and connection.

If I tamp down on my own response out of concern that I'll be creating too much separation from my partner ("autonomy betrays connection"), that makes this positive experience less likely. If I go to the opposite extreme and insist on making my partner's opinion wrong, this, too, won't serve the relationship, for reasons that will become more clear in the next chapters.

Last but not least, you can consciously seek to create a culture—a Tiny Country of two—that equally honors autonomy and connection. While the details will vary from partner to partner and from relationship to relationship, here are some possible strategies:

• Keep a sharp eye out for the Romantic Fallacy and pursue behaviors and activities that reinforce the partners' experience of autonomy.

• Identify counter-productive narratives about autonomy and connection and work in partnership to right (and re-write) them. Let's say Sam has internalized the "autonomy as betrayal" syndrome. He also happens to have sexual fantasies about women who aren't his partner because, well, he's human. He feels guilty about these fantasies because the story he tells himself is that this means he doesn't love his partner Jess. Although it's asking a lot of them, Sam and Jess can address this issue by agreeing to have Sam share a private fantasy about other women. Jess is a fair-skinned brunette and Sam goes into detail telling her about a fantasy tryst with a blonde and a Latina. In the dyad of his relationship, Sam is re-learning an important lesson: it's okay to be attracted to other women. By helping him re-write this script, Jill is providing perfect parenting. Or, more accurately, perfect re-parenting.

• Have non-judgmental conversations about the partners' needs for autonomy and connection. Structure activities to accommodate both partners' needs as fully and fairly as possible.

These Tiny Country conversations take place in what I call the Conscious Café, or alternatively the I-and-I Café.

But I'm getting ahead of myself. This is the stuff of the next chapter.

CHAPTER 3:

The Continuum of Connection

THE PARADISE PROJECT MODEL IS BASED ON CONNECTION (OR ITS AB-SENCE). The model places on a continuum five chambers, which I also call rooms, domains, spaces and stations. (There's no "right" word: use whichever works best for you.) The chambers range from utter isolation to complete connection. The former is the experience of hell, the latter the experience of heaven.

I seem to have drawn my notion of heaven and hell from the same source as the Rolling Stones' Keith Richards, who writes:

> *I've never found heaven ... a particularly interesting place to go. In fact, I take the view that God, in his infinite wisdom, didn't bother to spring for two joints—heaven and hell. They're the same place, but heaven is when you get everything you want and you meet Mummy and Daddy and your best friends and you all have a hug and a kiss and play your harps. Hell is the same place—no fire and brimstone—but they just all pass by and don't see you. There's nothing, no recognition. You're waving, "It's me, your father," but you're invisible. You're on a cloud, you've got your harp, but you can't play with nobody because they don't see you. That's hell.*

Connected = heaven. Alone = hell.

Peak experiences of ecstatic union can give us a taste of heaven. Deep depression can take us into hell. So can painful relationship experiences, especially when the bond of connection feels severed beyond repair.

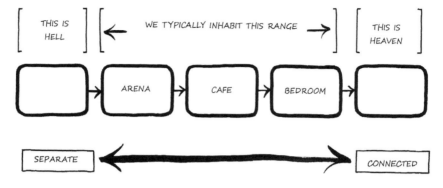

The Usual Range of Experience

For the most part, though, we cycle among the three middle stations—
the Courtroom (closest to hell), Café (the 'middle of the middle') and
Bedroom (closest to heaven).

The Arena

It's a jungle out there—sort of. More accurately, it's complicated out
there. It's also a courteous competition, a collaborative system, a tender
heart space and an ecstatic dance out there. But the jungle analogy still
has merit, somewhere beneath it all. With its connotation of savage
brutality, it reminds us that we're born alone and die alone, and that
during our time on this planet we must struggle to survive.

The Arena is where we engage this challenge and strive to make our
way in the world. It's the Jungle with some basic rules attached. Whereas
the jungle (as per Alfred, Lord Tennyson) is "red in tooth and claw" and has
only one rule, survival of the fittest, arenas are built by people and corralled
by laws.* It's competitive and sometimes confrontational and unpleasant,
but you can't rape and kill in the Arena and assume it'll be okay.

Biologists are now finding that ecosystems are built on cooperation as much as competition, so the old 'red in tooth and claw' view is losing much of its bite.

34

"Arena" evokes the Coliseum with its battles to the death along with a broader range of lower-stake activities—the sporting arena, the debate hall, the classroom, social climbing, the so-called free marketplace. A common denominator characterizes all these places: they're competitive environments. We participate, at least in part, to make our way, assert our claim or prevail. The Arena is where I express my unique identity, where I stand forward and proclaim, "This is me." Behavior in the Arena is ego-driven. It's not just about autonomy, it's about autono-ME.

Because it's ego-based, the Arena is about assertion, not connection. Behavior there takes separation for granted and doesn't seek to reduce it. The Arena thus supports and indeed requires dualistic thinking—*I'm like this and you're like that*—as well as judging—*I'm better at this than you.*

The Arena isn't intimate or heart-centered. These qualities are reserved for the Bedroom, which is two chambers away on the continuum of connection. Remember the autonomy-connection dyad? The Arena is home to autonomy, the Bedroom to connection. The Arena is where the toddler (now an adult) operates, on its own away from mom and her promise of intimacy. It's where we butt heads in the rough-and-tumble (but still mostly civilized) world.

Even though it can be an unappetizing place, we mustn't be judgmental about the Land o' Judgment. The Arena plays a crucial role inside our psyches and more broadly inside society, too. We need norms; we need to know (or, at least, believe we know) what's right and wrong, what's up and down. Even those of us who aspire to come solely from a heart-centered place of peace, love and understanding spend lots of time in the Arena. We all differentiate; we all judge. The Arena is an aspect of being human.

The Arena contains two chambers. The first I call Independence Hall. It's where we spread our wings, where we show up as artists or entrepreneurs or in whatever other way calls forth our self-expression. It's a good place because self-assertion is by and large a good thing—it goes hand-in-hand with joyousness, self-celebration and the spirit of adventure.

Intimate partners benefit from spending time in Independence Hall. If they don't, they won't feel whole, fulfilled or free. They'll feel tied to their partner's apron strings and their sense of autono-ME! will suffer.

(And their sex lives too, probably.)

The second chamber is the Courtroom. Understood in the usual sense, a courtroom is where legal claims are adjudicated. In the Arena, it's where ego claims are adjudicated. Some sort of conflict-resolution mechanism is a must in an environment like the Arena where people's competing opinions and judgments are constantly facing off against each other.

In the Arena, it's my claims against yours, my opinion against yours. A friend calls this mode of interacting the "Opine Forest." *I'm right. No, I'm right.* The Arena thus revolves around "right" in two senses. It produces competing claims about what is true, correct or ethically appropriate—about what *is* right—and also about what I'm entitled to—what's *mine* by right. Transactions in the Arena regularly surface issues of justice, equity and fairness.

Which is why a Courtroom is required.

Our inner Courtroom reflects many aspects of our secular judicial system. It's premised on the litigation model, which posits that the best way to arrive at a fair decision is through an adversarial process that pits an accuser against a defendant with the goal of producing a winner and a loser. It's built on the warfare model, with argumentation and persuasion instead of swords and guns. You prevail by winning points, by making your side look good and the other side look bad. The litigation model thus perpetuates the spirit of the Arena where it's ego versus ego in a context that's about competition, not collaboration.

We also internalize the litigation model's cast of characters. We walk about with a prosecuting attorney, defense counsel, and judge chattering away inside our heads. *I'm a bad person for being turned on by my partner's close friend*—that's the prosecutor. *But he's so hot I can't help myself!* The defense attorney. *For now, not guilty—but you'd better not fantasize about him* *while you're having sex with your partner!* The judge. We couldn't shut off these auto-pilot voices if we wanted to.*

These archetypes inhabit our psyches for good reason. They're there to help us work through the complex emotional and ethical issues that are constantly arising as we journey through our lives. So long as we spend time in the Arena (and who doesn't?), the prosecutor, defense attorney and judge will be our traveling companions and characters in our internal dialogues.

The litigation model is wildly ill-suited for conflict resolution between couples. How so? Let me count the ways.

First, as we've seen, the context is adversarial, with the goal of producing a winner and a loser. This approach works fine in some contexts, but intimate relationships aren't one of them. When couples quarrel, it's counter-productive to produce a winner and loser: that only breeds resentment and a sense of unfairness. Empathetic understanding needs to be the goal, with the resulting opening of the heart hopefully producing voluntary behavior change. The conflict-resolution process needs to bring the partners closer and the opposite usually happens with litigation.

Second, in real courtrooms there are laws of procedure and evidence that have emerged over the course of centuries to produce impartial outcomes. Collectively, these rules minimize bias and disorder and create a structure that allows the litigants to present their cases logically and coherently. They create order in the Courtroom. In relationship disputes, these rules are nowhere to be seen. When couples argue, they can say whatever they want, whenever they want, however they want. They can interrupt willy-nilly.

---

* The notion that we have many voices or personalities inside us has many schools and adherents. Eric Berne's Transactional Analysis proposes that we all have an inner parent, adult and child. Hal and Sidra Stone's Voice Dialogue approach has an inner guardian, an inner censor, and many other voices. Richard Schwartz's Internal Family Systems approach was developed in response to clients' descriptions of experiencing various parts—many extreme—within themselves. Poets have latched onto this notion, too. Michael McClure: "I am not a self, I am a congress of selves." Walt Whitman: "I contain multitudes."

There's no independent third party to make them toe the line or have the remarks struck from the record.

Third, there's no independent arbiter. Instead you get two internalized judges who come to the proceeding carrying the baggage of ancient stories, don't know what the rules are and communicate badly if at all.

Fourth, the evidence is as suspect as the judges. It, too, comes wrapped in ancient narratives and may not be objective.

Fifth, the prosecutor is often also the judge. *I accuse you and find you guilty!* This is the stuff of a kangaroo court, only in the case of domestic disputes, you've got a separate-and-equal judge/prosecutor across the way going all kangaroo back atcha.

Sixth, the voices inside our head are unpredictable: there's a squirrely inconsistency of direction. Sometimes the prosecutor turns on the person whose body they're inhabiting. *Yes, she had an affair, but honestly, you deserved to have her cheat on you—when was the last time you really paid attention to her?* It's as if the plaintiff's attorney had too many martinis at lunch and suddenly lays into their client.

Seventh, it's the aggrieved parties and not their representatives who are doing the arguing. Imagine if, in a real courtroom, you let the furious plaintiff face off against the furious defender instead of having their lawyers do the talking. It would degenerate quickly into Theater of the Absurd. Which is what happens with domestic arguments, pretty much every time.

Eighth—as if seven weren't enough!—the process itself triggers more grievances, unhappiness and hostility. Intimate partners go down the litigation path because one of them has a grievance. What they're hoping for is empathy—they want to come out of the conversation feeling understood. Litigation takes the participants in the opposite direction and leaves them feeling more alienated, more aggrieved and less understood.

LYNN (accusingly): You didn't clean the kitty litter today or yesterday. You know that's something you're supposed to do!

PAT: Geez, you're such a nag! Is nagging me one of your chores? And when was the last time you turned the lights off behind you? We're not made of money, you know!

LYNN: That's SO not relevant to why I started this conversation!

PAT: Well, it's relevant to me. And why did you start the conversation anyway? Because the cat wasn't around to kick?

LYNN: There you go, exaggerating again! I'm not kicking you, I'm asking you.

PAT: You didn't ask. You complained. From on high, like you're the perfect person! People who live in glass houses, you know what I'm saying? So why don't you just back off?

By the time the partners have traveled a few clicks down this highway, neither feels heard and both have their cranky-pants on.*

When couples litigate their grievances without the controls of a real-world courtroom, they create a negative feedback loop as one unloving communication begets another—the system is designed for degeneration. When this happens, the meta-message is one of hostility and your partner (and theoretical Beloved) acquires the status of enemy. The result: you go into fight-or-flight mode and do what it takes to protect yourself. You go on the attack; you suppress your capacity for empathy; you listen to make the other person wrong. To put it gently, these aren't effective conflict-resolution strategies.

Most of us are unskilled at conflict resolution. This is to be expected, given that conflict resolution isn't part of our basic education. Litigation is what comes naturally, all the more so if I'm angry or upset. When I'm feeling triggered, it feels right and appropriate for me to lay my grievance at your door in a manner that will make you fully aware of the pain you're causing me. I'm acting as my advocate, serving as my own public defender. This is righteous behavior, as seen through my eyes: since when is it wrong

---

* Cranky-pants: I learned this amusing and useful term from a friend who was babysitting a complaining toddler. "Ah, you have your cranky-pants on!" she noted. Cranky-pants: they're not just for little people.

to come to the aid of a victim of injustice, namely me? Beyond that, since when is it wrong for me to express my autonomy, to communicate in no uncertain terms my experience of the world and, more specifically, you?

The results are predictable. I'll probably get a hard-assed prosecutor coming back at me rather than the capitulation my aggrieved spirit is hankering for. A couple rounds of this and you've got two people with their cranky-pants pulled up around their ears while they lob missiles at each other and don't hear a word the other is saying.

The alternative to fighting is fleeing. In arguments, this takes the form of, *That's it, I'm done.* Or, in a marginally milder variant on the theme: *If you don't change, I'm out of here.*

In a gentler, more caring mood, you wouldn't be so harsh with your partner. Nor would you make threats you probably don't intend to act on. In the Courtroom, your own needs take priority: it's where self-assertion is your Prime Directive, even at the expense of your partner's feelings. The permission system of the Courtroom makes it okay to say and do things that would be off limits in a less "me first" place. Keeping the peace matters less than saying one's piece and claiming one's place.

This is why we tend to shoot our mouth off during an argument when we know better. The energy that's driving us is the energy of self-assertion. The energy of autonomy. And these trump caring and compassion.

Couples who deal with conflict in this manner create grave problems for themselves. The hostility gets embedded; the sense of not being heard or understood, along with the sense of not having one's autonomy appreciated, calcifies; and eventually you start to resent and ultimately hate your partner and the relationship. Hate's a big word, but it's not inappropriate here. When the pain of unsuccessful litigation gets wired into a relationship, when you get locked into that hard place of separation, you're teetering on the edge of absolute aloneness. You're on the verge of becoming the Still Face baby and this is a terrifying place. You're confronting the prospect of an imminent descent into hell, and so you react with hatred directed at the Beloved for putting you in that precarious position.

Many couples spend lots of time in the Courtroom or at its door. They're constantly feeling hyper-vigilant, finding fault, pressing the point that they're right while their partner's wrong and on the lookout for evidence that their partner is unworthy or that their partner finds them unworthy. It's not a happy situation, but for many it has payoffs. For one thing, it means you're not alone. Bad strokes can be better than no strokes, after all, and loud arguments do communicate that there's caring under there somewhere. Otherwise, why bother with all that sound and fury? In addition, when you're litigating, you're experiencing your autonomy: you're sticking up for yourself and that can feel righteous and good.

You're also feeling *something* and that can be better than feeling nothing at all.

No relationship is without its issues or points of contention. There will always be conflicts that require resolution. There will also usually arise, at some point, the desire to give your partner the smack-down they richly deserve—and that your autonomy would celebrate giving. How you manage these moments makes all the difference in a relationship. One thing is certain: if you litigate in the Courtroom, you're using a wildly ineffective tool for conflict resolution and opening a Pandora's box of negative emotions that will drag your relationship in the wrong direction.

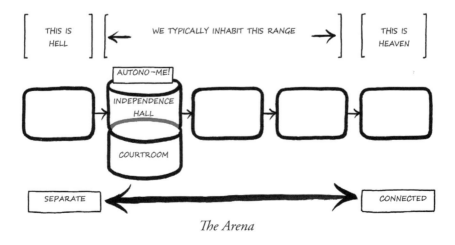

The Arena

The Bedroom

Now let's jump up to the Bedroom, which is separated from the Arena by the Café. Sexual intimacy is only one aspect of what happens here. More broadly, it's about the heart—the open, vulnerable, loving heart. When I am in close physical proximity to another person, it means one of two things. Either I'm in fighting mode and getting in the other person's face, or I'm in tender mode and bathing in the other person's energy field. The Bedroom is when we're in "tender mode," when we are energetically, emotionally and often physically close to our partner.

The Bedroom is not a world without judgment. It's there, but on the margins. It's experienced as irrelevant because the judging impulse is trumped by heart energy. When we're in the Bedroom, the soul says, "Why judge when we can love?" Tenderness and compassion are the dominant emotions.

The Bedroom is where couples bond, where they make that special connection. It's home to lovers or more precisely to lover *energy*, because they may or may not be having sex. The difference between friends and lovers is that the Bedroom is essentially off limits to friends: it's simply not done, or if it is done, it means that the line between friend and lover has become blurred.

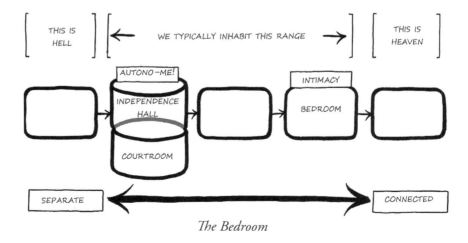

The Bedroom

Like the Arena, the Bedroom has a shadow, albeit a subtle one. The experience of being in the Bedroom can be so powerful that we want to be there all the time. It can, in other words, cause us to embrace the Romantic Fallacy, where we downplay or disregard our need for autonomy. We become the toddler who only wants to be with Mom and suppresses our urge to have adventures in the world. When we do this, we do ourselves a disservice and behave in ways that can also be annoying to the "Mom" of the moment, who has autonomy needs of his or her own and may not want us attached at the hip.

The so-called Sensitive New Age Guy, or SNAG, falls into this trap. He's so intent on connecting with the object of his affection that he neglects his own autonomy and hers as well. And then wonders why he's not getting the love, respect and sex his post-machismo sensitivity merits.

To sum up, the Bedroom is home to lovers, whether or not they're being sexual. The impulse to judge is overridden by the power of the open heart. The level of separateness is modest and the level of connection is high. The core drives, to borrow from Elvis Costello, are peace, love, and understanding.

The Bedroom's shadow arises directly from its appeal. It's so beguiling, so alluring, that we can come to want it all the time and lose sight of our need for autonomy.

The Café

The Café stands midway between the Arena and the Bedroom. It's where we courteously exchange views and information. It's where we choose to be civil with each other; it's the alternative to the hostility and aggression that can come from asserting one's claims in unbridled Courtroom-style fashion. The Café is the antidote to the Arena's shadow. Its norms keep the powerful from doing whatever they want to the weaker and more vulnerable.

How do we migrate our transactions into the Café? We suspend judgment and replace it by inquiry or, at a minimum, courtesy. If we have a negative opinion about what another person is saying, in the Café we may choose not to share it, or if we do speak up, we do so diplomatically.

In the Café, people are nice. Or pretend to be.

The Café is where we go to get along. It's where we choose to tamp down on all that Arena autono-ME! energy. It's where we check our egos at the door. We do this for the sake of community and harmony—and also, more fundamentally, because feeling safe feels good and the Café offers sanctuary relative to the ongoing threats of the Arena. Autonomy, as expressed in the Café, is kinder and gentler than the Arena version. The Prime Directive is to be civil and considerate, not to prevail. It operates on the premise that no one has special access to the truth and that everyone's perspective merits consideration.

Just as the Bedroom is for lovers, the Café is for friends. At the same time, though, it's important for romantic partners to spend time together in the Cafe. The best relationships are ones where your partner is both your lover and your friend. Thus partners need to spend time in both the Bedroom and in the Café—and in Independence Hall as well.

* * *

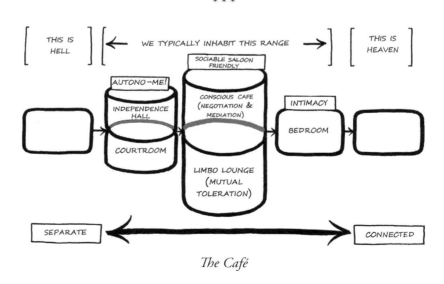

The Café

There are three distinct levels in the Café—think of it as having a ground floor, a mezzanine and an upper storey.

The lowest level is the Limbo Lounge. In Dante's *Inferno*, limbo was an anteroom to hell. People went there who hadn't done anything bad enough to merit being consigned to hell, but hadn't done anything worthy enough to earn them heaven, either. People in limbo were eternally unhappy, but not in total agony.

In relationships, couples that have spent too much time in the adversarial energy of the Courtroom often make their home in the Limbo Lounge. It's preferable to open warfare, but the civility is superficial. The Limbo Lounge is where unhappy couples keep a lid on it. They get along in the Limbo Lounge, but the silence behind the civility is fraught with the arguments that aren't happening, the grievances that are going unaired, the longing for intimacy they're not getting. The Limbo Lounge is where broken hearts go to not mend.

If these couples could spend more time in the Bedroom, it might undo some of the pain of their Courtroom transactions and raise their relationship center of gravity to a happier place on the continuum of connection. Unfortunately, the more time you spend in the Courtroom, the more difficult it becomes to find the heart connection that makes Bedroom interactions possible. The Limbo Lounge thus becomes a sort of mournful best-case scenario, where you're not in the Courtroom, bruised and battered and confronting the possibility of a Still Face future, but still feeling unhappy and unfulfilled.

The upper level I call The Sociable Saloon (or, if you have an issue with liquor, the Sociable Salon). It's where we go to have fun, to relax, to make connections. We're not talking Bedroom intimacy here: the Sociable Saloon is more easygoing, less intense. It's where people share good times together. Unlike the Limbo Lounge, it doesn't carry the shadow of the Courtroom around its neck. It's not a counterpoint to danger—it's where you hang out with folks in an easy, fun way that affirms your membership in the tribe.

Between the Limbo Lounge and the Sociable Saloon is the Conscious Café.* It's where we go to address grievances, resolve conflict, negotiate fresh understandings, and do the work of Tiny Country Creation. Like the Limbo Lounge, it exists as a counterpoint to the Courtroom. If I have a grievance but don't want to litigate it in the Courtroom, I will invite my partner to join me for a constructive conversation in the Conscious Café. If I'm concerned that my partner will respond in a way that will put me in my cranky-pants, I invite him to join me in the Conscious Café as a way of notifying him that some special interpersonal handling will be needed here. If I want to do some Tiny Country Creation—let's say I want permission to share all my sexual fantasies with my partner, which I haven't done yet—I'll invite her to join me in the Conscious Café, where the process that unfolds will be careful and controlled and much less likely to degenerate than without that call to awareness.

In the Conscious Café, there are specific rules of communication. The general requirements, as laid out in myriad relationship books, include the following:

- Empathetic listening

- Mirroring the partner's words until the partner feels genuinely heard

- Identifying the meanings you attribute to your partner's behavior as stories you're telling yourself, not the objective truth about what's going on. When we get into "This is what happened," "No, this is what happened!" arguments, we're in the Courtroom asserting our claims. When, instead, we limit our truth claims to the meaning we're ascribing to events, we're no longer claiming to know better than our partner—we're leaving the truth space open, so to speak.

---

* The Conscious Café isn't universal. Many people never spend time there. Thus we can view the Conscious Café as a sort of add-on, constructed by conscious couples to complement the basic Café duo of Limbo Lounge and Sociable Saloon.

- Responding only 'non-violently' (the term is Marshall Rosenberg's)—no attacking, no criticizing, no counter-complaining, no non-dealing, for instance by responding to your partner's story with a parallel story of your own ("That reminds me of when …").

- Staying "relational" (couples therapist Terrence Real's term), by which he means, essentially, staying in respectful relationship with your partner, even though your triggered self may want to shut them out (by putting up high boundaries) or put them down (by assuming a one-up, "I know better" position).

These protocols don't come naturally: we need to practice them until they become second nature.

The difference between the Courtroom and the Conscious Café is the difference between litigation and mediation. In litigation, our goal is to prevail. In mediation, our goal is to find a fair middle ground. Litigation is win-lose. Mediation is win-win. Litigation is adversarial and about winning points. Mediation is gentler, more compassionate, more civil. It has more heart in it, as is appropriate for a domain that's midway between the Courtroom and the Bedroom.

Let's say I feel treated unfairly: that will leave me with a grievance. This is a labor-law term, but its origins are in the heart: I grieve, therefore I have a grievance. What are my options in this case? I can file a complaint with my partner, i.e., undertake to litigate the matter. I can withdraw and withhold: I can, in other words, go on strike (the French word for "strike" happens to be *grève*, a close cousin to grieve). As we have seen, these are the usual responses: fight or flight, neither of which, in the relationship context, is effective.

There's a third way, though. I can take my grievance to the Conscious Café where the partners address it in a spirit of mediation, not via the strategies of litigation or passive-aggressive withholding.

I have an alternative name to the Conscious Café—the "I-and-I Café." The phrase "I-and-I" comes out of the Rastafarian tradition. It assumes that you and I are not separate beings. "I and I" and "you and me" are one and the same, seen from a perspective that fully embraces the oneness we all share.

If my partner and I disagree about something, we can view this disagreement through an ego-based lens that sees my belief, and your belief, and the gap between. But what if your belief were actually my belief too and I just didn't realize it? What if all your beliefs inhabited me somewhere? What if the conversation between you and me was actually a conversation between me and me (oops, 'I and I')?

For some people, stripping away the worldview that keeps our egos separate and replacing it with one that says, "You and I are one" makes it easier to be empathetic and emotionally receptive. If you're "over there," you may be my enemy. If you are me, or an aspect of me, you're on my side and I can safely let my guard down.

The spiritual teacher Byron Katie invites people, when they have a complaint about their partner ("Jill doesn't listen to me"), to reverse it ("I don't listen to Jill"). More often than not, she notes, this statement will be true. It's the "I-and-I" principle, shining in a mirror brightly.

The Limbo Lounge isn't a happy place: its only virtue is that at least the partners aren't shredding each other in the Courtroom. The vibe is much more positive in the Sociable Saloon. Hanging out with people, enjoying their company, interacting in community—these are good things. Joyous things. The spirit of play is present in The Sociable Saloon, and play is great for couples, for the simple reason that people who play together tend to enjoy each other's company. Time spent in the Sociable Saloon can dissipate Limbo Lounge energy quickly.

As for the Conscious Café, whether that's fun depends on the attitude you bring to it. When Lynn says to Brett, "I'd love to meet you in the Conscious Café for a conversation about your mother-in-law," if Brett's response is one of dread—if he views it as essentially an invitation to a Courtroom conversation in sheep's clothing—then it won't be fun for him. But if he views it as an opportunity to develop an important skill set—the skills of conscious communication—while also getting more connected with his partner—then his heart might open at the thought.

In the Conscious Café you're playing to win, not in the adversarial Courtroom sense of individuals pitted against each other, but as collaborators seeking a win for the relationship. *How skilled can we be at this? How skilled can we help each other be at this?* To what extent can we model right relationship? Once you get past its shadow—the perils of litigious Courtroom interactions—the Conscious Café soffers couples a really fun collaborative opportunity to transform the relationship into all it can be.

Tiny Country Creation: it's fun!

To sum up, the Limbo Lounge is about mutual toleration against the harsh background of Courtroom unhappiness. The Conscious Café emphasizes negotiation and mediation and is a mature alternative to the litigious Courtroom style. The Sociable Saloon is where we go to have fun, lightly.

Finding Your Relationship Center

Relationships tend to have a center of gravity. It's a function of where couples spend their time with each other. In the early madly-in-love stage, the center of gravity tends to be the Bedroom. Then, when the love chemicals

THE IDEAL CENTER OF GRAVITY

FOR COUPLES IS BETWEEN

THE CAFÉ AND THE BEDROOM.

and the glow of early-stage projection wear off, they discover (or invent) what's wrong with their partner and the picture. This can easily usher in an extended bout of Courtroom crankiness, born of dashed expectations, which in turn can lead to a relationship whose center of gravity is between the Courtroom and the Limbo Lounge.

Not pretty.

The ideal center of gravity for couples is between the Café and the Bedroom. This foundation is built out of time spent together as friends and time spent together as lovers, along with lots of fun, and little or no time as Courtroom combatants.

The Meadow

The human experience isn't limited to the three middle chambers. There are more extreme experiences, both good and bad.

Let's start with the positive—the experience of ecstasy, of "heaven." I've called this the Meadow, which makes sense when you know its origin, a wonderful short poem by the medieval mystic poet Rumi: *Out beyond notions of right and wrong, there's a meadow/I'll meet you there.*

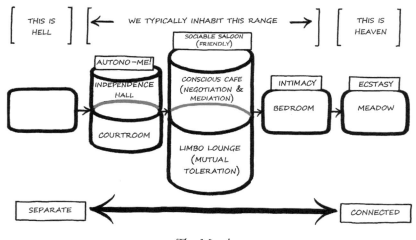

The Meadow

In the Meadow, all boundaries are dissolved. There is only the perfect unity of you and me and the universe we inhabit. Everything is right with the world—everything. This is because we've gotten past our dualistic illusions and are fully inhabiting a paradise of unbounded connection. We are cells in the world's perfect body.

Recall that in the Café, judgment is suspended, while in the Bedroom, judgment is swept away in the flow of heart-feeling. The Meadow takes this one step further. It's a truly judgment-free zone. *Out beyond notions of right and wrong.* The Meadow literally has no place for the discriminating mind. Instead we get perfect connection.

We all have the potential to experience the Meadow: heaven is hardwired into our DNA. We also all yearn for it: the Meadow is the foundational bliss and enlightenment experience. It's also what couples long for. It's the universe as maternal breast, with all things perfect just as they are.

The Dungeon

The flip side of heaven is hell, called here the Dungeon. It's an appropriate term for three reasons. It's a form of imprisonment (in this case, psychic imprisonment). It's also where we're incarcerated before we're brought to trial (or after) and thus a sort of anteroom to the Courtroom. Finally, it's a place of solitude and deep suffering. Kinky people make light of this and turn "dungeons" into play spaces, but any dungeon truly worthy of the name is a place of profound torment.

The Dungeon is home to perfect agony and thus the mirror image of heaven's perfect ecstasy. There's nothing redeeming about being in the Dungeon. It's a place of total separateness, total outcastness, total rejection. It is a paranoid, claustrophobic and literally hateful place. Just as everything about the world is right in heaven, here everything is wrong. The universe is toxic inside and out. Whereas the Meadow offers unconditional affirmation, the Dungeon delivers unconditional negation. Existence is experienced as a universal "no." In the Dungeon, judgment is absolute and absolutely painful—it brings punishment,

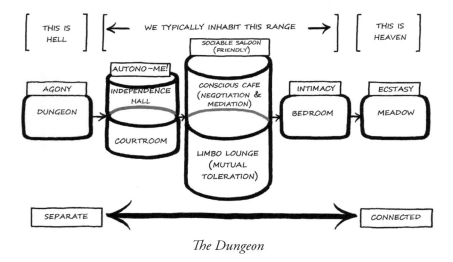

The Dungeon

pain and condemnation. The level of separateness is total and the level of connection non-existent. In the Dungeon, we are exiles from the kingdom, unworthy, unaccepted, alone. Remember the Still Face Project and how the infant was so quickly rendered hysterical by the abrupt severing of connection with its mother? That was the baby on a turbo tumble to the terrible aloneness of the Dungeon.

Once we become attached to another person, the Dungeon becomes one of our possible futures. If that person leaves us, whether by choice or death, we will have to navigate the horror of that abrupt severing of ties. We are all Still Face babies, potentially.

CHAPTER 4:

You Must Remember This

So now we have a map and a model. What's next? We apply it using six simple principles.

THE SIX PRINCIPLES

1. Do the Work (or, The Play's the Thing)

2. Know Which Room You're In

3. Don't Litigate in the Courtroom

4. e-L-evate Your Game

5. Be Proactively Positive

6. Be the Other's Light-Bearer

Principle #1: Do the Work (or, The Play's the Thing)

Improvement doesn't happen without effort. A significant commitment is required—a commitment that establishes itself at a level that makes change possible. We all know how it is: we resolve to improve ourselves, maybe by losing weight or stopping smoking, but somehow it doesn't quite happen. The commitment is only skin-deep. It hasn't made its way into the will, which is the only way real change happens.*

---

* A separate school of thought proposes that the most effective way to produce behavior change is by creating an inner environment that supports healthy decision-making without requiring the exercise of the will. For most people, though, will is what finds them a way.

There's good and bad news in this. First, the bad news: it can be very challenging to activate the part of yourself that allows meaningful change to happen. There's a lot of built-in resistance, or maybe it's orneriness or laziness. The good news is that, once you've climbed this mountain, you may be surprised to discover that the most difficult work is behind you. There will still be challenges, but you will find that the winds have shifted and that the Force is now with you. Once that steely resolve locks into place, it tends to be relentless. You're in charge now. You know you can overcome.

So what is the "work" you're required to do? As we've seen, it starts off with making a soul commitment—with resolving, ideally but not necessarily in collaboration with your partner, to follow the recommendations of the Paradise Project program. You don't need to make a lifetime commitment: we're not starting a church here. Resolve to try it for three or six months, or for whatever term of time you believe will be a fair test.

Next, you have to *remember* the commitment. Duh!, right? But getting caught up in daily distractions is a trap most of us fall into. *I'm going gluten-free but that pasta was so tempting. I'm stopping smoking but one cigarette after a couple of martinis isn't going to make a difference.* Doing the work means not forgetting you made the commitment. Your resolve has to be strong enough to not succumb to the inevitable temptations. You need to pay attention and keep paying attention.

Perfection isn't required here. You'll probably have episodes of forgetfulness. Forgive yourself when this happens and get back on the horse.

Over time, as these behaviors become habitual, remembering the program will become less of a problem. The good thing about habits is that they become habitual: you just do them.

"Doing the work" can and should be fun. The Paradise Project is a game, a word I use in two senses. It's behavior based on mutually agreed-upon rules. That's true for checkers, it's true for chess, and it's true for the Paradise Project, too. It's also a game in the sense that games are what kids play. They're entered into voluntarily, and they're fun. If the "work" is experienced as work, in other words as an unpleasant obligation, you can bet that one or both partners will abandon the project, probably sooner than later. By engaging the Paradise Project in a spirit of co-creation, we bring child energy into our undertaking and keep our creative juices flowing.

Fun matters. It *really* matters. And while, as we shall see, Paradise Project work has its challenging moments, for the most part it can be a really fun game the partners play together.

Now let's dig deeper and examine what "doing the work" (or, if you prefer, "playing the game") means.

It means embracing these six principles as fully as you can. It means living them, breathing them, making them second nature.

It means choosing mediation over litigation—the Conscious Café over the Courtroom.

It means doing your best to view Conscious Café dialogues as fun. It means celebrating yourself and your partner for having the courage and imagination to do the work of Tiny Country Creation.

Doing the work means choosing to make the entire endeavor fun. This is the game of relationship you're playing here, and one way you win is by having fun playing it. Realistically, you won't have fun all the time. Painful emotions will inevitably arise. Remembering your commitment to have fun can accelerate how fast those bad feelings dissipate.

Last but not least, "doing the work" means *growing against the grain* (a variant on going against the grain). This is where the going gets tough: this won't always feel like fun. Sometimes we need to step out of our comfort zone to grow. It may be fun and easy for me to hunker down in front of the television night after night instead of doing something more constructive like cooking a fine dinner or doing tantric breathing exercises. While I'd much rather be a masterful cook or skilled ecstatic lover than an Olympian TV-watcher, that doesn't make it any easier for me to rouse myself from my torpor. Still, it's there, in the direction of discomfort, where the opportunity for growth and self-improvement lies.

Sometimes we need to give ourselves a good ol' kick in the behind. Or our partner does.

We slip into comfort zones in relationships, too. As the sex therapist Esther Perel has observed, this often takes the form of a comfortable connection that comes with a diminishment of one's autonomous erotic impulses. As with watching television, it's really easy to stay hunkered down in the crib of shared comfort and convenience. But that's a form of entrapment: the partners are swapping security for aliveness. In Homer's *Ulysses*, Circe lures his sailors onto an island and turns them into swine— they become comfortable and unconscious. Something similar happens in relationships when couples fall asleep in the comfort of each other's companionship and allow the sense of freedom and autonomy that created all those sparks to wither on the vine.

Awakening each other's autonomy from within the comfort of relationship doesn't come naturally or easily. It requires us to *grow against the grain*.

Doing the work requires us to assess how we're doing at managing the balance between autonomy and connection and to take corrective measures when they're called for. It also requires us to do the difficult and sometimes painful work of trying to improve aspects of ourselves that are problematic for the relationship. If I learned from my parents to maintain a discreet silence when someone discusses their feelings, it can be painful to learn how hurtful my non-responsiveness is to my partner. If my kissing skills aren't what my partner wishes they were, it can be difficult to hear this, and hard not to feel ashamed when undergoing remedial kissing training. These are examples of work that needs to be done, examples of growing against the grain.

Principle #2: Know Which Room You're In

It's useful to make a practice of knowing where you are on the continuum of connection. Are you being quarrelsome? Do you have your cranky-pants on? Is irritability the mood music of the moment? You're probably dealing with thwarted desires and at the bench in the Courtroom. Are you in armistice mode? Are the conversations you're having weighed down by the thunderclouds of conversations you're not having? The Limbo Lounge. Are you having a conscious conversation about Something That Matters? The Conscious Café. Are things easy, painless, fun? The Sociable Saloon. Are you feeling tender, close, connected? The Bedroom.

You'll also want to know your partner's station. Notice if they're being litigious; notice if they're feeling tender and loving. As a practical matter, this is as much about paying attention to yourself as it is about paying attention to them. If your partner is in the Courtroom and you're not, you'll probably contract emotionally. (Unless you're also in the Courtroom, in which case you might welcome their crankiness as a fine excuse to go to war.)

Similarly, if your partner is gazing at you tenderly, your heart will probably open for the simple reason that love begets love.

So: know which room you're in—and, if the situations calls for it, do something about it. If your partner's in the Courtroom, you might share what you're sensing ("You seem upset and angry. Would you like to join me in the Conscious Café and talk about it?"). If she's in the Bedroom, you might want to kiss her and tell her you love her. Or throw him onto the bed and we'll let our imaginations do the rest.

Whatever the particulars, the key is—pay attention to the emotional energetics that you and your partner are feel-

THE PARADISE PROJECT IS A PRACTICE.

ing and that are being expressed in the co-created field of your relationship. *What room are you in? What room is your partner in?* If you consistently pay attention to this and take remedial action when necessary, you can make a grand success of the Paradise Project. If not, fuggedaboudit.

The Paradise Project is a practice. It requires you to practice paying attention, to practice being aware of what you are feeling and what your partner appears to be feeling.

"Paying attention to feelings" is not the same as getting caught up in your feelings. There's no merit in creating melodrama gratuitously. Nor is it the same as giving full faith and credit to the story behind your feelings, i.e., assuming that your feelings prove something beyond the fact that you're feeling what you're feeling. When Joe comes home with the proverbial lipstick on his collar, the only truth his partner Mary can know with certainty is that she feels agitated and upset. A Conscious Café conversation would go something like this—"When I saw that you had lipstick on your collar, the story I told myself was that you'd been fooling around with Denise."* While this formulation sounds less authentic than "You've been cheating on me, you son of a bitch!", it's preferable for two reasons. First, it stays on the right side of the boundary that separates *beliefs* about what's true from *claims* about what is true. Unlikely though it is, Joe may have gotten that lipstick stain from his octogenarian Aunt Matilda: Mary doesn't know for sure, and it's better for a host of reasons if she doesn't make that leap of logic. Second, it steers clear of the Courtroom. Feeling stilted and inauthentic is sometimes the price we pay for that. It's worth it.

Once you know what room you're in, the next step is to do something about it, assuming you want to shift the energy. In the Courtroom and feeling litigious? Your impulse is probably to press your claim. This is only natural—grievances want a hearing and fairness wants its day. You'll need to override this and that's not easy when you're riding the horse of righteous indignation and it's accelerating into a Kentucky Derby gallop. How do you put a stop to this? The heart won't help: it shows up here as self-love and is fully on the side of self-expression. There's only one way to bring the horse to a halt, and that's through an act of will. Of intention. You hold onto that piece of yourself that remembers that you know better—that the short-term gratification of self-expression will be more than outweighed by the inevitable relationship hangover the next day. And so you propose a visit to the Conscious Café. You grow against the grain, knowing that only dismounting will save the day.

---

* At this point it's pretty much conventional wisdom among couples therapists that this is the best way to frame difficult communications. Harville Hendrix and Terrence Real are among the therapists who recommend this approach.

Migrating from the Café to the Bedroom requires an act of surrender, not will. Making the transition from friend energy to lover energy requires an opening of the heart. You can't elect to do this like you can elect not to litigate in the Courtroom. The heart has its own rules that operate independently of what the mind instructs. Still, there are ways to get that recalcitrant heart to open. Eye-gazing is one strategy. What sex therapist David Schnarch calls "hugging till relaxed" is another. This is just what it sounds like: the partners hold each other until their anxiety dissipates and they're quietly present with each other. Spiritual exercises in which you see your partner as a perfected being, or alternatively choose to see their unperfected selves through a lens of unadulterated compassion, are other ways to get that vulnerable heart to open.

But all this begins with knowing which room you're in.

With paying attention.

Principle #3: Don't Litigate in the Courtroom

Litigating in the Courtroom is the Great Destroyer of relationships. The problem doesn't lie only with what's said, though that can get pretty ugly. It's also energetic. Hostility, impatience, disdain, dislike—emotions like these are like atomizers. Once released into the air, they tend to linger, and even after they've dissipated there's a residue that settles over the combatants. Negative emotions worm into our unconscious and over time undermine love.

Lord knows it's tempting to litigate in the Courtroom. If my partner has activated one of my wounds—if, in other words, I find myself with a grievance—it's natural to want to communicate my unhappiness in an authentic, straightforward way, and since I'm wearing my cranky-pants, that probably means complainingly and litigiously. Paradoxically, the urge to do so sometimes emerges from a deep faith in one's partner. *Since he loves me, that means he supports my autonomy and wants me to express my feelings authentically. Thus I'm in service to him and to the relationship by telling him what a jerk he is!*

This is toddler logic. Temper-tantrum logic. *If I throw a fit and mama doesn't abandon me, that'll prove she loves me.* So I'll scream really loudly, because the louder I scream, the more it'll prove she loves me if she's still there when I'm done. There is a perverse logic here, but it's one you'll want to steer clear of in a mature relationship.

Act on your understandable impulse to share when you have your Courtroom cranky-pants on, and you're basically getting in a car, flooring it, and driving off a cliff while feeling totally in control.

An alternative approach might go like this:

TOM: I'm starting to feel pretty triggered by this conversation. I'm concerned that I'm going to start going into litigation mode soon. Would you join me in the Conscious Café so I can deal appropriately with what's I'm feeling?

PAT: I'd love to do that, but now's not a good time. Can we schedule the conversation for this evening?

TOM: It won't be easy—there's a lot of stuff up for me right now—but if that's the first time you're available, it'll have to do. Thanks for being willing to join me in the Conscious Café.

PAT: I'm looking forward to it! It's a way for us to affirm to each other how skilled we are at the art of relationship and that we're masters at the art of Tiny Country Creation!

At which point the burden falls on Tom to calm himself as best he can until he can rendezvous with Pat in the Conscious Café.

In laying this down as what amounts to a commandment ("Thou shalt not litigate in the Courtroom"), I'm taking sides in a longstanding debate about communicating anger in a relationship. Is it appropriate to express one's anger angrily? The trajectory of couples counselors Harville Hendrix and his wife Helen LaKelly Hunt on this question is instructive. For a time, they advocated the open expression of anger. One partner would create a safe space for the other to ventilate. The notion here was that if you could get your feelings out and feel heard in the process, then you'd put your unhappiness behind you and could get on with your life and relationship unencumbered. But then Hendrix and Hunt started studying brain science and came to the conclusion that expressing anger angrily carves out neural pathways that make it more difficult to feel love and tenderness for your partner. Negative emotions become hardwired: your brain views your partner with fear and mistrust even if you want it to do otherwise. Thus neuroscience trumped the "ventilation" model of the psyche and Hendrix and Hunt became ardent advocates of the "no dumping of anger, ever" school of relationship well-being.

My stance on this issue is libertarian. It's up to each couple to decide what will work best for them. Some couples may find it useful to create a safe space in the Conscious Café for the expression of anger. Others may prefer to steer clear of anger entirely. Different strokes for different folks. And different Tiny Countries for different couples.

But this is detailing. The fundamental thing still applies: don't litigate in the Courtroom.

In other words, practice safe communication.

LITIGATING IN THE COURTROOM
IS THE GREAT DESTROYER OF RELATIONSHIPS.

Principle #4: E-L-evate Your Game

The "L" has priority here, for reasons that will soon be clear.

We've seen that one of the goals (or games) of the Paradise Project is to migrate the relationship center of gravity from south of the Café to between the Café and the Bedroom. How to accomplish this? In a phrase: through the pursuit of delight. The neurochemicals of pleasure, radiating throughout our bodies, are what send us climbing the stairway to heaven.

Delight (or, more humbly, fun) wears many masks. We experience it, among other things, as excitement (the roller coaster ride we're crazy enough to pay for), as wonder (the grace of the panther, the beauty of a coral community), as connection (eyes meeting over a glass of wine), as learning (the universe is an infinite library of fascinating stuff we don't know), as laughter (which, among many other benefits, releases feel-good endorphins), and of course as sensual delight (the whisper of breath, the touch of flesh).

To make these easier to remember, I've divided these experiences into three categories: love, laughter and learning. This is why the "L" in "e-L-evate your game" is accentuated: these are three "L's" we have here.

Every time you love, laugh and learn together, you are serving yourselves and your relationship. It will be even better if you do so consciously. Every time you enjoy one of the three "L's" together, you're doing great work in the Land of Tiny Country Creation.

> EVERY TIME YOU LOVE, LAUGH OR LEARN TOGETHER, YOU ARE SERVING YOURSELVES AND YOUR RELATIONSHIP.

Needless to say, these aren't the only ways to strengthen one's relationship. Seeing a tearjerker together doesn't fall under love, laughter or learning, but it can be a great way to spend time together if that's what you both enjoy.

The three L's aren't prescriptive. Feel free to create your own Tiny Country list of what ignites those positive vi-bra-tions for you. (A friend suggested lust and licking.) The broader point is this: there are feel-good neurochemicals and there are feel-bad neurochemicals. Relationships feed these systems. They create delight and desire: they also create stress and distress. The Paradise Project game calls for us to feed the good neurochemical system more and the bad neurochemical system less. When you love, laugh or learn with your partner, you're generating feel-good chemicals and sending the elevator up toward heaven. Litigating in the Courtroom or simply acting pissy or withdrawn generates feel-bad chemicals and sends the elevator in the wrong direction.

Don't take this to mean you should avoid dealing with difficult feelings. There will be times when you'll want to go to the Conscious Café to talk an issue through. You may not want to exercise this option every time, though. The magic of the Conscious Café lies in its capacity to transform animosity into a shared learning experience. It's an indispensable way for partners to e-L-evate their game. But there's an alternative. If you're feeling unhappy with your partner, you may want to propose watching *A Fish Named Wanda* instead. By the time you've finished laughing together, all those positive neurochemicals may have created such an airtight seal against the past that you've totally forgotten what you were angry about.

Conscious Café? We doan need no stinkin' Conscious Café!

Get those positive neurochemicals pumping. Love. Laugh. Learn. E-L-evate your game.

Principle #5: Be Proactively Positive

This principle is closely tied to the previous one. Feel-good chemicals aren't only generated by what we do. They're also generated by how we treat each other—and, just as importantly, by how we treat ourselves. Inside our heads, we have good stories about ourselves, and bad ones too. They're constantly yammering at us, and for many of us, it's the bad stories, which typically date back to our early childhood, that run the show. The more we inhabit these bad stories, the likelier we are to project them onto our circumstances. If I don't like myself, sooner or later I'll find myself not liking my partner, too.

There are ways to counteract this. Internally, we can note when negative tapes are playing and activate kinder, gentler ones. In our relationships, we can choose to communicate appreciation to our partner, not only in those moments when we feel inspired to do so, but as a matter of ongoing commitment—as an aspect of doing the work.

That's what this principle is about—undermining those ancient negative tapes by being proactively positive. Let's say your partner blurts out something irritable because the house is messier than she'd like. One option would be to say, "Feeling bitchy, are we?" A better choice would be, "I really appreciate you for how much you value having a clean house. Now may I invite you to frame your unhappiness a bit differently?"

Being proactively positive has multiple benefits. For starters, it gets me actively seeking out the positive. It points me in the direction of being appreciative and grateful, of having a compass for what's good about life. Ultimately this will track back on myself and I'll start seeing the positive in myself, too.

It also helps rewire my partner's tape. There's a part of the brain which believes that what it's told is true. If I think, "I'm in danger," the brain will start manufacturing fight-or-flight chemicals whether or not the danger is real. If I tell my brain, "Carl, you're an embarrassment," the brain will start pumping out chemicals associated with stress and shame, even if I'm lying alone in a hammock. By being proactively positive, we deluge our partner's brain—and our own—with positive stories. Eventually this drowns out the negative ones and we become happier and more fun people who are better able to spend our time on the sunny side of the street. And this, as we've seen, takes us up the continuum of connection.

At the end of the day—at the end of the rainbow—it's really simple. Negative takes us toward hell. Positive takes us toward heaven.*

You might want to try this simple exercise: Take negative judgments and frame them so they're positive. The person formerly known as a coward becomes someone 'with a strong instinct for self-preservation.' Your liar becomes someone 'with a gift for narrative flexibility.' A judgmental bitch becomes a person with a 'powerful critical faculty.' There's comedy here, to be sure, but the overarching point is a serious one: Accentuate the positive. Always.

Being proactively positive can feel inauthentic at first. This isn't surprising: you're developing a new habit. Do it anyway. In fact, do it to excess—and then examine the reasons for your discomfort, assuming you're feeling any. Why are you feeling skittish about actively looking for and celebrating the goodness, beauty and talent in your partner? Do you believe you're diminishing yourself in elevating him? Are you afraid she'll get a swelled head and dump you because she'll decide you're unworthy? Are you worried he'll view you as a sycophant? Whatever the reasons for your hesitation, override them. The more important point is that you're doing the important work of Tiny Country Creation. You're re-wiring your partner's brain and your own. You're firing up the feel-good chemicals that will make it easier for you and your partner to delight in life and each other. It's never a bad thing to say "Hallelujah!"

You might even want to make a game of it. Can you spend an hour together and have every exchange include a thank you or appreciation about your partner? How about a whole day? Can you play the game in front of friends and do so unabashedly?

The term "making love" is usually thought of in the context of sex. That's too limited. When we're playing the "proactive positivity" game, we're making love in the sense that we're literally manufacturing it. We're generating love's feel-good chemicals, appreciation by appreciation.

Which brings us to that word: 'appreciate.' It has two meanings—"see a positive quality" and "rise in value." The two meanings converge here.

---

* The prominent psychologist John Gottman has done extensive research that confirms the hypothesis that kindness breeds togetherness while criticism drives couples apart. In one study, Gottman found that the four negative behaviors that most predict divorce are criticism of partners' personality, contempt (from a position of superiority), defensiveness and stonewalling (or emotional withdrawal). On the other hand, couples most likely to stay together are generally supportive of each other and handle conflict in a gentle, positive manner.

The more we appreciate our partner, the more the quality of our relationship appreciates.

There's a simple principle at work here. The more time you spend in positive territory with your partner, the better off you and your partner will be. The more time you spend in negative territory, the worse off the two of you will be. Seems obvious, no? Yet it's a truth that often eludes our vision. What we're discussing here is a dividing line that the great myths have been addressing since time immemorial. It's the divide between good and evil, positive and negative, the Force and the Dark Side.

Each of us has the power to choose which side of the divide we want to be on, both as an individual and in the dyad of our relationship. Nothing requires us to be run by our Dark-Side stories or by habitual negative modes of interacting. We have the power at any given moment to choose the light.

In fact, we can do even better than that. By being proactively positive, we alchemically transform darkness into light.

Principle #6: Be The Other's Light-Bearer
Let's summarize our guidance so far:

1. Make a commitment (Principle #1: Do the work).

2. Pay attention (Principle #2: Know which room you're in).

3. Just say no to feel-bad chemicals
   (Principle #3: Don't litigate in the Courtroom)

4. Flood your partner and yourself with feel-good chemicals
   (Principle #4, e-L-evate your game, and Principle #5, Be proactively positive).

One last step is missing here. Help each other out. Support each other. It's easy to fall off the Paradise Project wagon, for instance by getting caught up in negative thinking and Courtroom complaining: old habits die hard, after all. As one of the covenants in your Tiny Country, you might want to have an understanding that if one of you backslides, the other is authorized to gently and lovingly point that out.

There's an important secret buried in this book. At the end of the day, the Paradise Project isn't about having a happier *relationship*. It's about having a happier you. You do this by steering clear of feel-bad chemicals while actively pursuing feel-good ones. While it's great for couples to do this together, this is ultimately a personal and private journey. When you make the conscious decision to "marry" your feel-good chemicals and "divorce" your feel-bad ones, you're embarking on a spiritual journey that can product dramatic positive transformations. You don't need to be in a relationship to do this.

> THE PARADISE PROJECT ISN'T ABOUT HAVING A HAPPIER RELATIONSHIP. IT'S ABOUT HAVING A HAPPIER YOU.

I'll illustrate this with a personal story. As I was writing this chapter, I was in my car hoping to make a light, and the driver ahead of me was dawdling. I responded with impatience and irritation. "What's wrong with this person? Don't they understand that when you drive, you're in community and you have to be aware of the other drivers, too?"

The moment I noticed my reflexive intolerance, I realized something else as well. When I'm behind the wheel, I'm constantly bathing myself in feel-bad chemicals. If another driver falls short of the mark, I'm all over them Courtroom-style, albeit only in my head.

In that moment of insight, it was blindingly clear to me that there are better ways for me to expend my emotional energy when driving. Instead of punching the clock in the Courtroom-chemical manufacturing plant, I could choose to practice compassion. A few minutes later, I got trapped behind another dawdler. This time, I imagined that they were feeling distressed, which is why they were driving so distractedly. It felt better. I felt better. I had crossed over to the feel-good side of the street.

Being proactively positive is a life skill and not strictly speaking a relationship skill, though it can be invaluable in your relationships.

When we serve as our partner's light-bearer, we are supporting them on their independent, autonomous journey toward happiness and fulfillment. This is one of the greatest gifts a friend can give a friend.

Conveniently, when we do this, we also benefit ourselves—it was Ralph Waldo Emerson who wrote, "It is one of the most beautiful compensations of this life that no man can sincerely try to help another without also helping himself." Every reminder to our partner is also a reminder to our own self. Any time we help our partner stay on the Paradise Project path, we're doing the relationship—and ourselves—a service.

To be sure, being the other's light-bearer is tricky. Trying to be your partner's coach will probably end badly, and trying to be your partner's therapist is pretty much guaranteed to. You and your partner need to establish clear boundaries about what is and is not appropriate "light-bearer" behavior. When is it okay to speak up? How often is it okay to speak up? How should the comment be framed? Light-bearer interventions can easily be experienced as intrusive and resented. You want to love, support and be a role model for your partner, but you never want to be a nag. Nor do you want to get in the habit of being on the lookout for your partner's falling short of the mark. When you set up shop in the critical zone, you're hunkering down in the Courtroom. You're manufacturing feel-bad chemicals.

When you're your partner's light-bearer, you need to bear light, and be light. No darkness or heaviness, please! Remember Principle #5: be proactively positive.

* * *

Conceived as a game and ongoing collaboration, the Paradise Project holds out the promise of a wonderful reward—a life in harmony with a dear friend and best beloved; a life led in the ongoing certainty that, as per the Beatles, it's getting better all the time; a life where fun (lots of it!) is interspersed with episodes of profound, ecstatic connection.

When you do the Paradise Project, you're in service—to yourself, to your partner, and more broadly to the spirit of goodness in the world. You're on the side of the angels in a journey into celebration. You're creating beauty—emotional beauty, spiritual beauty—feel-good chemical by chemical.

Sounds a lot like paradise to me.

Continuum of Connection Chart

	DUNGEON	**COURTROOM**
ROLE OF JUDGMENT	Absolute	Central
LEVEL OF SEPARATENESS	Total	High
LEVEL OF CONNECTION	Non-existent	Modest
GOAL	To survive	To successfully assert one's claim
CORE EMOTION	Horror	Self-assertion
CORE VIRTUE	None	Discrimination
CORE DRIVES	Reduction of suffering	Freedom, power, autonomy, self-expression
SHADOW	It is only shadow	Negativity (*you must lose for me to win*)
EPISTEMIC ORIENTATION	Paranoid (*only pain is true*)	Ego-centered (*my beliefs are true*)

CAFÉ	BEDROOM	MEADOW
Sidelined	Overridden	Non-existent
Moderate	Modest	Non-existent
Moderate	High	Total
To understand and be understood	Intimacy	No goals
Belonging	Caring	Bliss, gratitude
Open-minded inquiry	Tenderness & compassion	Being fully present
Learning & community	Devaluation of autonomy	Surrender
Erosion of sense of depth	Connection	None
Egalitarian *(all truths are created equal)*	Heart-centered *(what I feel is true)*	Non-dual *(no distinction between knowing and not-knowing—that's just another judgment)*

APPENDIX B:

Practices and Techniques

HERE ARE SOME ACTIVITIES Sheri and I do to keep our relationship on track.

General Continuous-Improvement Strategies

INTENTION STATEMENTS AND REVIEWS. Every morning, we share how we intend to engage the day and each other. A representative statement might be, "I intend to work on my book most of the day, get some exercise, and spend any extra time I have getting the utility room ready for painting. Whenever I feel stressed, I intend to breathe and let it go. As for our relationship, I intend to be proactively positive by volunteering at least one appreciation every hour. I will also share something fun or exciting that I learned over the course of the day." At night, we review how we did and discuss how we might do better.

THE APPRECIATION GAME. Go ahead, get crazy. How many positive, loving, appreciative things can you say about your partner? Go overboard in letting them know how much you appreciate them.

It's especially useful to do this when your partner expresses irritation or anxiety. It's a great way to transport them from a bad-chemical to a good-chemical place.

You can play this game in any number of ways—the only limit is your imagination. As per the example earlier on this page, you can commit to at least one appreciation per hour. You can have an appreciation accompany every transaction. ("We're out of eggs." "Thanks for noticing!

I really appreciate how you track our refrigerator inventory.") You can sit your partner down five times a day and share ways you love them (this is the Mecca version of the game). You can have a "Day of Living Positively," where the rule is that the partners can't say anything negative for the entire day. If one of the partners has that contracting feeling that tells them they've been spoken to negatively, they can ask for a do-over (see below) and their partner obliges without question.

If doing this feels uncomfortable, that's okay. Grow against the grain.

PERIODIC PERFORMANCE REVIEWS. I know: it sounds mighty corporate. Don't let that stop you—there's value in taking time out to note how the relationship is progressing over time. Where was the relationship center of gravity six months ago? Where is it now? Where would you like it to be? These are important questions. It makes sense to discuss them.

A-C-E MAPPING. Ideally, a performance review will include an examination of how the partner's autonomy, connection and equity (A-C-E) needs are being met. Is the relationship falling into the trap where the lust for autonomy is being stifled? Are the partners' needs for touch and sex being met? Do both partners feel that the relationship is fundamentally equitable? Are there grievances in this area? If so, they should be surfaced and addressed.

A-C-E Mapping needs to take place in the Conscious Café. Don't let them tumble into the Courtroom, which is an ongoing risk when suppressed grievances are given permission to emerge. Remember that these are collaborative exercises designed to produce best outcomes for both parties. You're co-creating something better here. Don't let them devolve into gripe sessions.

Courtroom Management Strategies
Even the most self-aware people sometimes get negative and litigious. Here are some ways to keep things from getting worse.

THE DO-OVER. Let's say your partner says something that triggers you. Or he's irritable with you for no apparent reason. One option is to respond in kind, in which case the chances are reasonably good you'll soon be off to the Courtroom races. There's a better way, though. You can request a do-over.

> AVON: Where are the light bulbs?
> BRETT: They're in the same place they were when you asked me yesterday.
> AVON: Ouch! May I have a do-over, please?
> BRETT: Sure. They're in the hall closet. And by the way, you asked me the same question yesterday.
> AVON: Thank you.

A variation on this is the scripted do-over. Imagine that, in the above example, Brett couldn't come up with phrasing that worked for Avon. The following conversation might ensue:

> AVON: Can we try a scripted do-over?
> BRETT: I guess we'll have to!
> AVON: Here's what I'd like you to say to me. 'They're in the hall closet. I guess you didn't hear me when I told you yesterday.'
> BRETT: They're in the hall closet. I guess you didn't hear me when I told you yesterday.
> AVON: Thank you.

The key with the scripted do-over is to repeat the words verbatim.

NAMING AND INVITING. If the do-over and scripted do-over don't do the trick, the next step is to name what's going on ("I'm sensing Courtroom energy here") and invite your partner to join you for a dialogue in the Conscious Café. This is a call to attention for both parties, a reminder of their intention to not litigate in the Courtroom.

PERFECT PARENTING. Let's say I'm feeling triggered. I say so and immediately my partner comes over and hugs and consoles me. We can think of this as do-over parenting. Child gets upset, Mom provides a heaping helping of perfect parenting.

This strategy is for advanced practitioners. Typically, if I'm feeling triggered, it will either be because I'm responding to my partner's being triggered, or it will in turn trigger my partner. The person playing the perfect parent must be able to put aside their negative feelings and be perfectly comforting and consoling. That's not easy.

INTERVENTIONS BORN OF DESPERATION. So now you're off to the races, deep into Courtroom hostilities. You both know that if you continue in this vein, things will only get worse. Couples and family therapist Terrence Real recommends two interventions when this happens:

  • The dead-stop contract is an agreement between the partners that, if one of them calls for a dead stop, the other will cease their behavior immediately whether or not they believe the person's request is merited.

  • Unlike the dead stop, which is a "you statement" ("you need to stop"), the time out is self-directed. Essentially, the time out signal means, "I have to end this conversation right now because if I don't, I might say something I'll regret." The time out comes with a time limit. A person can call a time out for 20 minutes, two hours, one day—whatever.

With both the dead stop and time out, an intervention occurs that breaks the downward spiral.

PHYSICAL EXERCISES. Couples can also shift energy using physical approaches. One example is the Emotional Freedom Technique (EFT), an acupressure-based technique that releases held emotions. Another is Monkey Breath, a chaotic breathing technique that scrambles brain patterns and shifts emotions. Other options include taking a walk or exercising vigorously.

Conscious Café Strategies

INQUIRY AND MIRRORING. Unless you're ready to dismiss your Courtroom quarrel as a transient shortage of blood sugar—and sometimes that's the best way to proceed—you'll eventually want to head with your partner toward the Conscious Café. Use it as a learning opportunity: it's a places where you can "e-L-evate your game." Ask questions and mirror back what your partner says. Stay humble. There's a gap between you two, otherwise you wouldn't have had that quarrel. It can take time to bridge it.

THE PARENT-CHILD GAME. This is a variant of the "Perfect Parenting" exercise described above. The person with the grievance takes the child role and their partner takes the parent role. The "child" then gets to express its feelings as a child would. The parent holds and comforts the child and communicates empathy and understanding. You can make your own Tiny Country agreement about the extent to which the expression of anger is permitted here.

TRIGGER POINT THERAPY. Trigger point therapy is a type of massage, but that's not how we mean it here. We all have specific triggers that activate old wounds. We can work with those triggers in the Conscious Café. Let's say Joe, who has heart disease, gets reactive every time his partner Joanne comments critically about his appetite for potato chips and ice cream. They could re-enact the triggering encounter in the Conscious Café with a view toward giving him an opportunity to observe his reaction, breathe into it, and learn to respond differently. During the course of this practice, Joanne might also learn to respond differently to Joe when she sees him eating in ways she believes are unhealthy.

What's happening here is that the partners are taking an issue that typically sends them into the Courtroom and bringing it into a sanctuary where they can learn to handle it more skilfully.

INTENTION/LEARNING STATEMENTS. You're on a learning journey with your partner. Use Conscious Café conversations as an opportunity to learn how to do it better. These lessons are likelier to be integrated if they're articulated. For this reason, we recommend sharing with your partner what you've learned from the Conscious Café conversation and how you intend to adjust your behavior in the future.

From Café to Bedroom
HUGGING TILL RELAXED. We alluded to this earlier: the partners hold each other until they feel safe and connected with each other.

EYE-GAZING. The partners gaze into each other's eyes and visualize the other as a perfected being, as a god or goddess. Or, in a variation, the partners view each other with compassion, envisioning their Beloved as a as flawed (yet perfect) being with fundamentally pure intentions.

THE 'I LOVE YOU' GAME. The partners eye-gaze and take turns saying, "I love you." At any time, either partner can switch to "You love me?" with variations on that theme. "You really love me?" "I really love you." And so on. This can be a great ice-breaker, especially if there's lingering Courtroom tension in the air.

TAKING A CHANCE. Sometimes there are topics we're afraid to broach and this shuts us down. When you take a chance, it doesn't always pay off—a risk is a risk—but it can also open the heart. Both partners' hearts.

BED ROOM NOW. The Bedroom has its own special energy. It's heartfelt and it's tender. When we go about our daily rounds, that energy tends to dissipate in the face of other priorities. We put on our business face, our parenting face, our friendly Sociable Saloon face. Our capacity for Bedroom energy goes on hold until we land in the Bedroom again, which may or may not be often.

Couples can shift this pattern with a mantra, "Bed Room Now," that's a variation on the meditation teacher Jon Kabat-Zinn's famous advice: "Be Here Now." It's a way for partners to remind themselves to bring intimate energy into their other times together. Not that they'll be lying alongside each other gazing into the other's eyes while standing in line at the bank—but they can choose to smile tenderly at each other or give their partner's hand a squeeze or do any of a thousand other little things that will evoke Bedroom tenderness.

We tend to lead emotionally segregated lives—either the Bedroom or another chamber. This is unfortunate not only because intimacy feels good, but also because Bedroom tenderness is the glue that holds relationships together. By playing the "Bed Room Now" game regularly, we can integrate our lives and live in love more often.

This is not a comprehensive list. The Paradise Project is open source. You are cordially invited to come up with your own activities—the only limit is your imagination.

Relationship is a game. A serious game, but a game. Ditto for Tiny Country Creation. So remember as best you can to stay positive and have fun. This won't be possible every minute, but if you remain committed to producing feel-good chemicals, more joy will come your way, and what's not to like about that? Joy is its own reward, and it comes with a bonus—it sends us up the continuum of connection.

There's a happiness principle at work here, which we can practice alone or in relationship.

If you want to get to heaven, you've got to go into delight.

* * * *

CARL FRANKEL is the managing director of
Sheri Winston's Center for the Intimate Arts. For more
information: IntimateArtsCenter.com, CarlFrankel.com.
To contact Carl directly: carl@carlfrankel.com.